Dutch Home Cooking Cookbook

Hearty Recipes and Sweet Treats from the Netherlands

By: Martha Stanford

© 2024 Martha Stanford, All Rights Reserved

Important Notice

Dear Valued Reader,

This book is the result of my hard work and dedication. I kindly ask that you respect my intellectual property rights by not reproducing, distributing, or transmitting any part of this publication in any form or by any means without my prior written consent. This includes photocopying, recording, or using electronic or mechanical methods. However, brief quotations used in critical reviews and certain other noncommercial uses are permitted by copyright law.

I have put a great deal of effort into ensuring that the information provided in this book is both accurate and useful. However, I cannot guarantee specific results or outcomes from applying this information, as individual circumstances may vary. It is important to remember that you have the power to make your own choices and determine the path that is right for you. While I hope that the content of this book will inspire and guide you, ultimately, the way you choose to use this information is up to you.

By reading this book, you acknowledge that I shall not be held responsible for any consequences resulting from the use or misuse of the information presented.

Thank you for your understanding and for respecting the time and effort I have put into creating this work.

Table of Contents

Introduction 5

Delight in Dutch Breakfast Favorites 7

   1. Dutch Ham & Cheese Egg Stack 8

   2. Dutch Apple Bacon Pancake 11

   3. Classic Dutch Mini-Pancakes 14

   4. Dutch-Style French Toast 17

   5. Groningen Morning Loaf 20

Hearty Dishes and Lighter Sides 23

   6. Dutch Beef Stew 24

   7. Chicken Skewers with Kick 27

   8. Dutch Egg Bombs 29

   9. Dutch Beef Stew 32

   10. Dutch Fries Delight 35

   11. Dutch-Indo Noodle Feast 38

   12. Smoked Eel Delight 41

   13. Dutch Currant Bread 43

   14. Dutch Pea Soup 46

   15. Crispy Mussel Bites 49

   16. Dutch Veggie Mash with Sausage 52

   17. Goat Stew Delight 55

18. Limburg Beef Stew 58

19. Beef and Apple Bake 61

20. Dutch Pork Pockets 64

21. Dutch Potato Salad 67

22. Mashed Potato Medley 70

23. Bacon-Hugged Meat rolls 73

24. Mustard Magic Soup 75

25. Cheesy Puff Pockets 78

Enjoy Delicious Dutch Desserts 80

26. Dutch Spice Cookies 81

27. Dutch Doughnuts 84

28. Brandied Apricots 87

29. Classic Dutch Almond Crisps 89

30. Dutch Almond Butter Cake 91

Conclusion 93

Introduction

Welcome to the world of Dutch cooking! In the Netherlands, food is an important part of daily life and culture. Dutch people typically eat 6-7 times a day, including 2-3 snacks between meals. Family dinners are a cherished tradition, with over 65% of Dutch families with children eating dinner together at home every day.

Dutch cuisine is a mix of simple, hearty dishes and international influences. While about 25% of meals include animal products, there's a growing trend towards vegetarian and vegan options, especially in cities. Sustainability is becoming more important in food choices.

Breakfast in the Netherlands is usually simple. Many people between 20 and 50 years old often skip it, while others grab a quick bite at home or on the go. Yogurt cups and breakfast bars are popular choices for busy mornings.

Lunch is a social affair, with sandwiches being a common choice. It's a time for relaxing and connecting with others.

Dinner is typically eaten at home with family. Dishes vary, but the focus is on spending quality time together after the meal.

In this cookbook, you'll find a range of recipes that reflect these Dutch eating habits. From quick breakfasts to hearty dinners, and plenty of snacks in between, these dishes will give you a taste of everyday life in the Netherlands. Whether you're cooking for yourself or gathering the family around the table, these recipes will help you bring a bit of Dutch flavor into your home.

So, roll up your sleeves and get ready to cook some delicious Dutch food. Your taste buds are in for a treat!

xxxxxxxxxxxxxxxxxxxxxx

Delight in Dutch Breakfast Favorites

xxxxxxxxxxxxxxxxxxxxxx

1. Dutch Ham & Cheese Egg Stack

This Dutch breakfast is a local favorite in the Netherlands. It's quick, tasty, and fills you up. The combo of fried eggs, ham, and cheese on bread is simple but hits the spot. It's perfect for busy mornings or lazy weekends. You'll love how easy it is to make and how good it tastes.

Preparation Time: 10 minutes

Serving size: 1 serving

Ingredients:

- 2 large eggs
- 2 slices white bread
- 2 slices shaved boiled ham
- 1 teaspoon unsalted butter
- 2 slices Gouda cheese (or any cheese you like)
- Kosher salt and ground pepper to taste

xxxxxxxxxxxxxxxxxxxxx

Instructions:

A. Melt the butter in a skillet over medium heat.
B. Crack the eggs into the skillet and let them fry until the bottoms set.
C. Take the pan off the heat and put a lid on it.
D. Let the eggs sit and steam for a minute or two until the tops firm up a bit.
E. While the eggs are cooking, toast the bread if you want.
F. Put the bread on a plate.
G. Place the fried eggs on top of the bread.
H. Layer the ham slices over the eggs.
I. Add the cheese slices on top of the ham.
J. Sprinkle some salt and pepper over everything.
K. Serve right away while it's still warm.

Special Notes:

- Try adding a thin layer of mustard on the bread before stacking the other ingredients. It adds a nice tangy kick to balance the rich flavors.
- For extra crunch, sprinkle some crushed potato chips on top of the cheese. It might sound weird, but it adds a fun texture and salty flavor that goes great with the eggs and ham.

2. Dutch Apple Bacon Pancake

This Dutch pancake is a breakfast favorite. It's a mix of sweet apples and salty bacon in a fluffy pancake. People love it because it's easy to make and tastes great. It's perfect for lazy weekend mornings when you want something special but don't want to spend hours cooking.

Preparation Time: 40 minutes

Serving size: 4 servings

Ingredients:

- 4 bacon strips, diced
- 1/2 cup shredded fontina cheese
- 3 large eggs
- 1/2 cup all-purpose flour
- 1/2 cup whole milk
- 1 1/2 teaspoons brown or Dijon mustard
- 1/4 teaspoon kosher salt
- 1/4 teaspoon ground pepper
- 3 tablespoons unsalted butter
- Fresh parsley, chopped (for garnish)

xxxxxxxxxxxxxxxxxxxxx

Instructions:

A. Cook the bacon in a heavy skillet over medium heat until crispy. Set aside on paper towels.
B. Shred the cheese and set aside.
C. Heat your oven to 425°F. Put the rack in the lower third.
D. Mix milk, flour, eggs, mustard, salt, and pepper in a bowl until smooth.
E. Wipe the skillet clean. Melt the butter in it over medium heat, coating the bottom and sides.
F. Pour the batter into the hot skillet.
G. Sprinkle the bacon and cheese in the middle, leaving a 1-inch border.
H. Bake for 15-17 minutes until the edges are brown and puffy.
I. Lower the oven to 325°F and cook for 3-5 more minutes until set.
J. Take it out, add parsley on top, cut into wedges, and serve hot.

Special Notes:

- For extra flavor, try adding thin apple slices to the bacon and cheese topping. The sweetness of the apple complements the salty bacon perfectly.
- If you're out of fontina, Gouda or Gruyère make great substitutes. They melt well and add a nice nutty flavor to the pancake.

3. Classic Dutch Mini-Pancakes

These small, puffy pancakes come from the Netherlands. They're a hit at breakfast tables and food markets. Made with regular and buckwheat flour, they get their fluffiness from yeast. You'll love how these little bites melt in your mouth!

Preparation Time: 1 hour 25 minutes

Serving size: 4

Ingredients:

- 1 cup buckwheat flour
- 1 cup all-purpose flour
- 2 large eggs
- 1 teaspoon instant yeast
- 1&1/3 cups warm milk
- 1 teaspoon granulated sugar
- 1/2 teaspoon kosher salt
- 1 tablespoon unsalted butter + extra for serving
- Optional toppings: powdered sugar, whipped cream, strawberries

xxxxxxxxxxxxxxxxxxxxxx

Instructions:

A. Mix 1 tablespoon of warm milk with yeast in a small bowl.
B. In a bigger bowl, mix flour, eggs, salt, sugar, and 1/2 cup warm milk.
C. Add yeast mix to the bowl. Whisk until smooth.
D. Pour in the rest of the milk. Whisk again.
E. Cover bowl with plastic wrap. Let's sit for 1 hour.
F. Melt butter in a pan. When it sizzles, drop small circles of batter to make tiny pancakes.
G. Flip when bottom sets. Cook the other side.
H. Serve with butter, sugar, cream, and berries if you want.

Special Notes:

- For extra flavor, try adding a pinch of cinnamon or vanilla extract to the batter.
- If you don't have buckwheat flour, you can use all regular flour. The taste will be different, but they'll still be yummy!

4. Dutch-Style French Toast

This Dutch twist on French toast is a breakfast favorite in the Netherlands. It's known for its super soft texture from soaking in a tasty egg mix. People love it because it's easy to make and tastes great with cinnamon and sugar on top. It's perfect for using up old bread too!

Preparation Time: 40 minutes

Serving size: 3 servings

Ingredients:

- 8 slices day-old white bread, crusts removed
- 1 & 1/2 cups milk (2% fat)
- 2 large eggs
- 2 tablespoons powdered sugar, plus 2 tablespoons for topping
- 1/2 teaspoon grated lemon zest
- 1/2 teaspoon vanilla extract
- 1/4 cup unsalted butter

For the Topping:

- 1/2 teaspoon ground cinnamon

xxxxxxxxxxxxxxxxxxxxx

Instructions:

A. Warm up the milk in the microwave for 30 seconds.
B. Mix eggs, 2 tablespoons powdered sugar, lemon zest, and vanilla into the warm milk.
C. Put the bread in a 9x13 inch dish. Pour the milk mix over it. Let it sit for 30 minutes until the bread soaks it all up.
D. Melt the butter in a big pan over medium-high heat.
E. Carefully move the soggy bread to the pan. It might fall apart, so be gentle.
F. Cook each side for 5-7 minutes until it's golden brown.
G. Put the cooked toast on a plate. Mix the rest of the powdered sugar with cinnamon and sprinkle it on top.
H. Serve and enjoy your Dutch-Style French Toast!

Special Notes:

- Try using brioche bread instead of white bread for an extra rich flavor.
- For a fun twist, add a splash of orange juice to the milk mixture. It gives a nice citrusy kick that goes well with the cinnamon sugar topping.

5. Groningen Morning Loaf

This breakfast cake from Groningen, Netherlands is a local favorite. It's a hearty mix of nuts and spices in a sweet loaf. Perfect with coffee, it'll fill you up and start your day right. The mix of flavors is addictive - you might find yourself making it for snacks too!

Preparation Time: 1 hour 55 minutes

Serving size: 1 loaf

Ingredients:

- 2 cups rye or wheat flour
- 1 teaspoon baking powder
- 1/2 cup brown sugar
- 1 pinch kosher salt
- 2/3 cup whole milk
- 1 & 1/3 cups unsalted mixed nuts (walnuts, cashews, almonds, etc.)
- Unsalted butter for greasing
- 2 teaspoons of spice blend (cinnamon, ginger, coriander, clove, nutmeg, etc.)

xxxxxxxxxxxxxxxxxxxxx

Instructions:

A. Set the oven to 275°F.
B. Mix flour, spices, baking powder, sugar, and salt in a bowl.
C. Pour in milk. Stir until you get a sticky mix.
D. Let it sit for 15-20 minutes.
E. Grease a loaf pan with butter.
F. Put half the nuts on the bottom of the pan.
G. Add the batter on top.
H. Sprinkle the rest of the nuts over the batter.
I. Bake for 1 hour and 15 minutes.
J. Take it out and enjoy!

Special Notes:

- Toast the nuts before adding them to the cake for extra crunch and flavor.
- Try swapping out 1/4 cup of the milk with strong coffee to give the cake a subtle coffee kick that pairs well with the nuts and spices.

Hearty Dishes and Lighter Sides

xxxxxxxxxxxxxxxxxxxxxx

6. Dutch Beef Stew

This Dutch beef stew is a classic comfort food from the Netherlands. It's a slow-cooked dish that turns tough meat into soft, pull-apart pieces. The mix of spices gives it a unique taste. It's perfect for cold days when you want something warm and filling.

Preparation Time: 4 ½ hours

Serving size: 4 servings

Ingredients:

- 2 lb. stew beef, cubed
- 3 ½ tablespoons unsalted butter
- 3 large onions, finely chopped
- 3 ¼ cups chicken or beef stock
- 4 whole cloves
- 3 fresh bay leaves
- 1 cinnamon stick
- 2 tablespoons vinegar
- 1 teaspoon juniper berries
- Kosher salt and ground pepper to taste

xxxxxxxxxxxxxxxxxxxxxx

Instructions:

A. Dry the beef with paper towels and cut it into cubes.
B. Melt the butter in a big pot over medium heat. Add the beef and cook until it's brown on all sides. Sprinkle with salt and pepper.
C. Toss in the chopped onions and cook until they turn golden and soft.
D. Pour in the stock and vinegar. Add the cloves, bay leaves, cinnamon stick, and juniper berries.
E. Turn up the heat and let it boil. Then, lower the heat, put a lid on the pot, and let it cook slowly for 3-4 hours. Check now and then and add water if needed.
F. The stew is ready when the meat falls apart easily and the liquid has turned into a thick sauce.
G. Before serving, fish out the cinnamon stick, bay leaves, cloves, and juniper berries you can see. Throw these away.
H. Serve hot and enjoy your Dutch beef stew!

Special Notes:

- For extra flavor, try adding a tablespoon of brown sugar or a splash of red wine to the stew while it's cooking.
- If you like your stew thicker, mix a tablespoon of cornstarch with cold water and stir it in near the end of cooking time.

7. Chicken Skewers with Kick

This Dutch take on Indonesian satay is super popular in the Netherlands. It's all about juicy chicken chunks on sticks, soaked in a spicy-sweet sauce. If you like meat on a stick and bold flavors, you'll love this. It's easy to make and great for parties or a quick dinner.

Preparation Time: 1 hour 20 minutes (plus 1 hour marinating)

Serving size: 12 servings

Ingredients:

- 1-pound boneless, skinless chicken breast, cut into cubes
- 4 cloves garlic, chopped
- 1/2 teaspoon ground coriander
- 2 tablespoons sambal bajak (Indonesian chili sauce)
- 1/4 cup ketjap manis (Indonesian sweet soy sauce)
- 1 tablespoon ketjap asin (Indonesian salty soy sauce)
- 2 tablespoons sunflower oil

xxxxxxxxxxxxxxxxxxxxxx

Instructions:

A. Mix chicken cubes with both soy sauces in a bowl.
B. Toss in garlic, chili sauce, and coriander. Stir well.
C. Cover and let sit in the fridge for 1 hour.
D. Thread chicken onto skewers.
E. Heat oil in a pan or grill.
F. Cook skewers until chicken is done, about 8-10 minutes.
G. Serve hot and enjoy!

Special Notes:

- For extra flavor, add a squeeze of lime juice to the marinade. The acid helps tenderize the chicken and gives a zesty kick.
- If you can't find Indonesian soy sauces, mix regular soy sauce with some brown sugar for ketjap manis, and use regular soy sauce for ketjap asin. It's not exactly the same, but it'll do in a pinch!

8. Dutch Egg Bombs

These egg balls are a Dutch snack sensation. Born in the Netherlands, they're a hot item at food stalls. Imagine a hard-boiled egg wrapped in spiced beef ragout, then fried to golden perfection. It's a savory treat that'll make your taste buds dance. Once you try one, you'll be hooked!

Preparation Time: 1 hour 15 minutes

Serving size: 4

Ingredients:

- 14 oz beef ragout
- 2 tsp fresh parsley, chopped
- 1 tsp Provencal herbs
- 2 tsp mild curry powder
- 1/2 tsp sweet paprika powder
- 1 cup + 5 tbsp all-purpose flour
- 5 large eggs (4 for boiling, 1 beaten)
- 1 cup breadcrumbs

xxxxxxxxxxxxxxxxxxxxxx

Instructions:

A. Boil 4 eggs until hard. Peel and set aside.
B. In a pan, mix ragout with herbs and spices. Heat it up.
C. Stir in 1 cup flour gradually over low heat until it's dough-like. Take it off the heat and let it cool.
D. Grab some foil squares. Spread ragout mix on each. Pop a hard-boiled egg in the middle. Wrap it up, making sure the egg is evenly covered.
E. Set up three plates: one with 5 tbsp flour, one with beaten egg, and one with breadcrumbs.
F. Unwrap each egg ball. Roll it in flour, then egg, then breadcrumbs.
G. Fry in oil at 350°F for 5-6 minutes. They're ready when golden brown.
H. Let them cool a bit, then dig in!

Special Notes:

- For extra crunch, mix some crushed potato chips into your breadcrumbs.
- Try swapping the beef ragout for chicken or veggie ragout for different flavors. The technique stays the same, but you'll get a whole new snack experience!

9. Dutch Beef Stew

This Dutch beef stew, or Hachée, is a hearty meal from the Middle Ages. It's popular in the Netherlands for good reason. The main stars are tender beef and sweet onions. You'll love how the meat falls apart and the rich flavors blend together. It's perfect for cold days.

Preparation Time: 3 hours 30 minutes

Serving size: 4 servings

Ingredients:

- 3 lbs. stew beef, cubed
- 3 large onions, chopped
- 2 tablespoons white flour
- 1 beef stock cube (about 0.25 oz)
- 75 oz unsalted butter
- 3 tablespoons red wine vinegar
- 4 fresh cloves
- 3 fresh bay leaves
- Kosher salt and black pepper to taste

xxxxxxxxxxxxxxxxxxxxxx

Instructions:

A. Melt butter in a big pot.
B. Add beef cubes and cook until brown. Take out and set aside.
C. Cook onions in the leftover fat until they turn see-through and slightly brown.
D. Put beef back in the pot and mix with onions.
E. Sprinkle flour over everything. Cook on low heat for 1-2 minutes, stirring often.
F. Pour in warm water just enough to barely cover the beef.
G. Add stock cube, vinegar, cloves, and bay leaves.
H. Cover the pot and let it simmer on low heat for 3 hours or more.
I. Taste and add salt and pepper as you like. Serve hot.

Special Notes:

- Secret flavor boost: Add a tablespoon of mustard to the stew for extra tang and depth.
- Texture trick: For a thicker stew, mash a boiled potato and stir it in near the end of cooking. It'll give a nice, creamy texture without changing the flavor too much.

10. Dutch Fries Delight

This Dutch Street food favorite is a tasty mess of fries topped with peanut sauce, mayo, and raw onions. It's popular at food stands and loved for its mix of flavors. The fries are crispy, and the toppings add a creamy, spicy kick. It's a fun, filling snack that's hard to resist.

Preparation Time: 50 minutes

Serving size: 4 servings

Ingredients:

For the satay sauce:

- 1 & 1/2 cups chicken broth
- 1 tablespoon sweet soy sauce (kecap manis)
- 1 tablespoon peanut oil
- 1 medium onion, finely chopped
- 2 garlic cloves, minced
- 2 teaspoons Indonesian spicy chili paste (sambal oelek)
- 1/2 teaspoon fresh grated ginger
- 1/2 cup creamy peanut butter
- 2 teaspoons dark brown sugar

For the fries:

- 4 large Russet potatoes
- Vegetable oil for frying
- Kosher salt to taste

For the topping:

- 3/4 cup mayonnaise
- 1/2 onion, finely chopped
- Ground pepper to taste

xxxxxxxxxxxxxxxxxxxxx

Instructions:

Make the satay sauce:

- A. Heat peanut oil in a pan. Cook chopped onion until soft.
- B. Add ginger, chili paste, and garlic. Cook for 1 minute.
- C. Stir in peanut butter, 3/4 cup chicken broth, brown sugar, and sweet soy sauce.
- D. Cook for 5-10 minutes. Cool and store in the fridge.

Prepare the fries:

- A. Peel and cut potatoes into fries. Soak in cold water, then dry.
- B. Heat oil to 325°F in a large pot.
- C. Fry potatoes in batches for 4-6 minutes until cooked.
- D. Drain on paper towels.

Serve:

- A. Put fries on a plate.
- B. Top with satay sauce, mayo, and chopped onions.
- C. Add pepper to taste.

Special Notes:

- For extra crunch, double-fry the potatoes. After the first fry, let them cool, then fry again at 375°F for 2-3 minutes.
- Try adding crushed peanuts on top for more texture and nutty flavor.

11. Dutch-Indo Noodle Feast

This Dutch-Indonesian dish blends East and West. It's a hit in the Netherlands, thanks to their colonial past. Packed with noodles, chicken, shrimp, and veggies, it's a tasty mix of flavors. You'll love how the sweet soy sauce ties it all together. It's comfort food with a twist!

Preparation Time: 50 minutes

Serving size: 4 servings

Ingredients:

- 12 oz bami noodles (or other Asian noodles)
- 2 large eggs, beaten
- 3 tablespoons vegetable oil
- 1 1/4 pounds chicken breasts, cut into 1/2" pieces
- 2 garlic cloves, minced
- 2 teaspoons ground coriander
- 1 teaspoon ground ginger
- 1/2 cup vegetable broth
- 1 medium onion, cut into wedges
- 1 carrot, thinly sliced
- 1 red pepper, thinly sliced
- 1 leek, thinly sliced
- 5 oz ham, cubed
- 5 oz raw shrimp
- 1 tablespoon chili paste
- 4-6 tablespoons Indonesian style sweet soy sauce
- Salt and pepper to taste

xxxxxxxxxxxxxxxxxxxxxxx

Instructions:

A. Cook the noodles as the package says. Drain and set aside.
B. Heat a big pan and spray it with cooking oil.
C. Pour in the eggs to make a thin omelet. Let it cool, then cut it into strips.
D. In the same pan, heat the oil. Cook the chicken with the broth, ginger, coriander, and garlic for about 6 minutes, until it's not pink anymore.
E. Throw in the onion, carrot, pepper, and leek. Cook for 5 minutes.
F. Add the ham, shrimp, and chili paste.
G. Cook until the shrimp turn pink, about 3-4 minutes.
H. Mix in the egg strips and noodles. Stir well and heat through.
I. Add the sweet soy sauce, salt, and pepper.
J. Give it a final stir and serve hot.

Special Notes:

- For extra crunch, toss in some crushed peanuts just before serving. It adds texture and a nutty flavor that goes great with the dish.
- If you can't find Indonesian sweet soy sauce, mix regular soy sauce with a bit of brown sugar or molasses. It'll give you a similar sweet and savory kick.

12. Smoked Eel Delight

Smoked eel is a Dutch favorite. Once common, now it's a treat because eels are harder to find. You'll see it at fish shops all over Amsterdam. It's salty, smoky, and rich. If you like fish, you'll probably enjoy this. It's easy to make at home if you can get fresh eels.

Preparation Time: 8 hours

Serving size: 4 servings

Ingredients:

- 2 lbs. fresh eels
- 2 cups salt
- 1 gallon filtered water

xxxxxxxxxxxxxxxxxxxxxx

Instructions:

A. Clean the eels. Scrape off the slime from their skin. Rinse them well.
B. Cut open the belly past the vent. Take out the guts and kidneys. Wash out any blood. Keep the heads on.
C. Mix salt and water to make brine. Soak eels in it for 2 hours.
D. Rinse eels again. Push sticks through them from the belly to behind the head.
E. Let eels dry for 1-2 hours.
F. Smoke eels at 140°F for about 3 hours. Lower heat once they start to firm up.
G. Check if they're done by pressing the sides. If the meat comes off the bone easily, they're ready.
H. Serve and enjoy your homemade smoked eel.

Special Notes:

- For extra flavor, add a mix of juniper berries and bay leaves to your smoker. This gives a nice woody taste to the eel.
- If you can't find fresh eel, try this method with trout or mackerel. They're oily fish that smoke well too.

13. Dutch Currant Bread

This Dutch treat is a hit at bakeries across the Netherlands. Packed with currants, raisins, and candied peel, it's a sweet bread that'll make your taste buds dance. Perfect for breakfast or as a snack, it's a must-try for anyone who loves fruit-filled baked goods.

Preparation Time: 3 hours 45 minutes

Serving Size: 16 servings

Ingredients:

- 3 & 1/2 cups dried currants
- 4 (1/4 oz) packages active dry yeast
- 2 teaspoons granulated sugar
- 1 cup lukewarm water
- 1/2 cup candied peel
- 3 cups raisins
- 7 1/4 cups bread flour
- 1 teaspoon ground cinnamon
- 1 cup whole milk, room temperature
- 2 large eggs
- 1 teaspoon kosher salt
- 2 teaspoons unsalted butter

xxxxxxxxxxxxxxxxxxxxx

Instructions:

A. Soak currants and raisins in warm water for 30 minutes.
B. Drain, dry, and mix with candied peel.
C. In a big bowl, mix flour and cinnamon. Make a hole in the center.
D. Add sugar and yeast. Pour in 1/4 cup warm water. Wait 5 minutes until it foams.
E. Add the rest of the water, eggs, milk, and salt. Mix into a dough.
F. On a floured surface, knead in the fruit mix for 5 minutes until smooth.
G. Put dough in a bowl, cover with a damp cloth. Let it grow for an hour in a warm spot.
H. Butter two 9x5 inch loaf pans. Shape dough into loaves, put in pans. Cover and let rise for 45 minutes.
I. Heat oven to 350°F (175°C).
J. Bake for 45 minutes until dark brown. Cool on a wire rack for an hour before slicing.

Special Notes:

- Try soaking the dried fruit in warm tea instead of water for an extra flavor kick.
- For a nuttier version, add 1/2 cup of chopped almonds to the dough when mixing in the fruit.

14. Dutch Pea Soup

This thick, hearty soup is a Dutch favorite. It's packed with pork, veggies, and split peas. People love it because it's filling and tasty. The soup gets better if you let it sit overnight. It's perfect for cold days when you need something warm and comforting.

Preparation Time: 35 minutes

Cooking Time: 7-8 hours

Serving Size: 8 servings

Ingredients:

- 1 (16 oz) package smoked sausage, sliced
- 1 (14 oz) bag dried split peas
- 1 whole ham hock
- 3 slices bacon, chopped
- 2 (14.5 oz) cans chicken broth
- 5 cups water + extra if needed
- 4 small potatoes, peeled and diced
- 2 carrots, peeled and diced
- 1 leek, diced
- 1/2 large onion, diced
- 2 celery stalks, diced (leaves chopped)
- 1 garlic clove, diced
- 1/2 teaspoon kosher salt
- 1/2 teaspoon dried thyme
- 1/2 teaspoon ground pepper
- 1/4 teaspoon ground cloves
- 1/2 teaspoon ground nutmeg

xxxxxxxxxxxxxxxxxxxxxx

Instructions:

A. Put the ham hock, bacon, and split peas in your slow cooker.
B. Pour in the chicken broth and water.
C. Cook on high for 3-4 hours. Stir now and then. Add more water if needed to prevent burning. The peas should break down and get soft.
D. Toss in the carrots, potatoes, onion, leek, garlic, and celery. Cover and cook on high for 2 more hours.
E. Add the salt, pepper, nutmeg, cloves, and thyme. Stir in the sliced sausage.
F. Cover and cook for 2 final hours to mix the flavors.
G. Serve hot and enjoy your Dutch pea soup!

Special Notes:

1. For extra richness, try adding a splash of cream or a dollop of sour cream when serving.
2. If you like a smoother soup, use an immersion blender to partially blend it before adding the sausage. This will make it even thicker and creamier.

15. Crispy Mussel Bites

This Dutch classic turns mussels into crispy, bite-sized treats. Popular in coastal towns, it's a fun twist on seafood. You'll love the crunchy outside and soft inside. It's perfect for sharing with friends or as a unique appetizer. The herbed mayo adds a tasty kick.

Preparation Time: 35 minutes

Serving size: 4 servings

Ingredients:

- 2&1/4 pounds mussels, cleaned and in shells
- 3 tablespoons olive oil
- 2 garlic cloves, finely chopped
- 1 parsley stalk, coarsely chopped
- 2 tablespoons dry white wine
- 3/4 cup all-purpose flour, sifted
- 4 large egg whites, beaten
- 1&1/2 cups panko or plain breadcrumbs
- Ground pepper, to taste
- Sea salt, to taste
- Herbed mayonnaise, as desired

xxxxxxxxxxxxxxxxxxxxxx

Instructions:

A. Heat olive oil in a pan over high heat. Add garlic and parsley. Sprinkle in some pepper. Stir well.
B. Pour in the wine and add the mussels. Cover the pan. Every 30 seconds, lift the lid and give the mussels a good shake to help them open.
C. Once most mussels have opened, take the pan off the heat. Scoop out the mussels and remove the meat from the shells. Throw away any unopened shells.
D. Let the mussel meat cool a bit. Set your deep fryer to 350°F (175°C).
E. Arrange 3 plates in a row. Put flour on the first, egg whites on the second, and breadcrumbs on the third.
F. Pat the mussel meat dry. Roll each piece in flour, then egg whites, and finally breadcrumbs.
G. Fry the coated mussels until they're light brown. Take them out and let them drain on paper towels.
H. Serve hot with herbed mayo on the side.

Special Notes:

- For extra crunch, try crushing some potato chips and mixing them with the breadcrumbs.
- Add a splash of lemon juice to the egg whites for a zesty twist that complements the mussels' flavor.

16. Dutch Veggie Mash with Sausage

This Dutch dish is a mix of mashed veggies and sausage. It's big in the Netherlands and easy to make. You'll love how the different veggies blend together. The sausage on top makes it filling. It's great for cold days when you want something warm and tasty.

Preparation Time: 45 minutes

Serving size: 6 servings

Ingredients:

- 2 lbs. potatoes, peeled
- 1 lb. butternut squash
- 1&1/2 lbs. Dutch sausage (or your favorite type)
- 8 oz sweet potatoes
- 3 large carrots
- 2 large parsnips
- 1 large turnip
- 1 large leek
- 1 medium onion
- 1 lb. cabbage (or kale or collard greens)
- 1/2 cup unsalted butter
- Kosher salt and ground pepper to taste

xxxxxxxxxxxxxxxxxxxxxx

Instructions:

A. Peel and chop the potatoes, squash, sweet potatoes, carrots, turnip, and parsnips.
B. Finely chop the onion.
C. Clean the cabbage and leek, then slice them.
D. Put all the veggies in a big pot. Add just enough water to cover them.
E. Cook on medium-high heat with the lid on until it boils.
F. Turn heat to medium-low and let it simmer for about 20 minutes until veggies are soft.
G. While veggies cook, prepare the sausage as the package says. Slice it and keep warm.
H. Drain the cooked veggies. Mash them, leaving some chunks if you like.
I. Add salt and pepper to your liking.
J. Mix in the butter well.
K. Put the sausage on top and serve.

Special Notes:

- Try roasting the butternut squash before adding it to the mash. It'll give a nice, sweet flavor.
- For a twist, add a handful of crispy bacon bits to the mash. It'll give extra crunch and saltiness.

17. Goat Stew Delight

This Dutch goat stew is a hit in the Netherlands. It's hearty and full of flavor. You can use goat or lamb meat, mixed with veggies and spices. It's perfect for cold days or when you want a filling meal. People love it because it's easy to make and tastes great.

Preparation Time: 2 hours 30 minutes

Serving size: 6-8 servings

Ingredients:

- 4 cups cool water
- 3 tablespoons fresh lime juice
- 2 lbs. goat or lamb meat, cubed
- 2 tablespoons canola oil
- 1 medium onion, diced
- 1 red bell pepper, diced
- 1 tablespoon no-salt-added tomato paste
- 1 cup water
- 1 tablespoon white vinegar
- 1 tablespoon sweet soy sauce
- 1 teaspoon ground nutmeg
- 1 teaspoon sweet paprika
- Kosher salt and ground pepper to taste

xxxxxxxxxxxxxxxxxxxxx

Instructions:

A. Mix meat with cool water and lime juice in a big bowl. Let it sit for 10-12 minutes.
B. Drain the meat and squeeze out extra water.
C. Heat oil in a large pan until it's very hot.
D. Cook meat for 6-8 minutes until brown.
E. Add pepper and onion. Cook for 2-3 minutes until the onion is soft.
F. Put in tomato paste, water, soy sauce, and vinegar.
G. Add nutmeg and paprika. Add salt and pepper as you like.
H. Turn heat to high and let it boil.
I. Lower heat, cover pan, and cook for about 1.5 hours. Stir now and then.
J. When meat is tender, it's ready to eat.

Special Notes:

- For extra flavor, try adding a bay leaf or two while the stew simmers.
- If you like it spicy, throw in a chopped jalapeno with the bell pepper and onion.

18. Limburg Beef Stew

This beef stew comes from Limburg, Netherlands. It's a local favorite that used to be made with horse meat but now uses beef. The stew is tangy and sweet, with a unique mix of vinegar and apple syrup. It's perfect for cold days and will warm you up in no time.

Preparation Time: 2 hours 35 minutes + 8 hours marinating time

Serving size: 4 servings

Ingredients:

- 2 lbs. shoulder beef steak
- 2 slices gingerbread
- 1 lb. onions
- 3 dried bay leaves
- 4 fresh cloves
- 4 tbsp apple syrup
- 1 cup white wine vinegar
- 1 cup filtered water
- Kosher salt to taste
- Oil for cooking, as needed

xxxxxxxxxxxxxxxxxxxxx

Instructions:

A. Cut the beef into chunks and put in a bowl.
B. Add water, vinegar, salt, cloves, and bay leaves. Mix well and let sit in the fridge overnight.
C. The next day, slice onions into half-rings.
D. Heat oil in a big pan and cook onions until soft.
E. Take the meat out of the marinade. Keep the marinade.
F. Add more salt to the meat if you want. Cook it in the pan until brown.
G. Pour in the marinade and apple syrup. Cook on low heat for 2 hours.
H. Break up the gingerbread and stir it in. Mix well and serve hot.

Special Notes:

- For extra flavor, try adding a splash of dark beer to the stew while it's cooking.
- If you can't find gingerbread, use a mix of molasses and brown sugar instead. It'll give a similar sweet and spicy taste.

19. Beef and Apple Bake

This Dutch dish warms you up on cold days. It's a mix of beef, apples, and potatoes that's popular in the Netherlands. People love it because it's easy to make and tastes great. You'll enjoy the sweet and savory combo in every bite.

Preparation Time: 40 minutes

Serving size: 4 servings

Ingredients:

- 8 oz onion, peeled and sliced
- 4 tablespoons unsalted butter
- 12 oz cooked beef, chopped finely
- 1 & 1/4 cups beef or chicken stock
- 4 cups mashed potatoes
- 2 medium Granny Smith apples, peeled and sliced
- 1 tablespoon breadcrumbs

xxxxxxxxxxxxxxxxxxxxxx

Instructions:

A. Turn on your oven to 375°F.
B. Grab a pan and melt 2 tablespoons of butter over medium heat.
C. Toss in the onions and cook them until they're golden. This should take about 8-10 minutes.
D. Add the beef and stock to the pan. Heat it all up.
E. Grease a baking dish with some butter.
F. Melt the rest of the butter in a small pot over low heat. Set it aside.
G. Start layering in the baking dish:
   - Put half the meat mix on the bottom
   - Spread half the mashed potatoes on top
   - Add all the apple slices
   - Add the rest of the meat
   - Top with the remaining potatoes
   - Sprinkle breadcrumbs over everything
   - Drizzle the melted butter on top
H. Bake for 15-20 minutes until it's hot and crispy on top.
I. Serve it up while it's hot!

Special Notes:

- Try adding a splash of apple cider to the beef mixture for extra flavor.
- For a crunchy twist, mix some crushed nuts with the breadcrumbs before topping the casserole.

20. Dutch Pork Pockets

\These tasty Dutch sausage rolls come from Brabant. They're a big hit in the Netherlands. Wrapped in soft dough, the spiced pork filling is the star. You'll love how the butter makes the bread extra good. Perfect for snacks or meals, they're sure to be a new favorite.

Preparation Time: 1 hour 30 minutes

Serving size: 10 servings

Ingredients:

- 2 cups all-purpose flour + extra for dusting
- 1/2 teaspoon granulated sugar
- 1 teaspoon instant yeast
- 1/2 cup whole milk
- 1/3 cup unsalted butter, softened
- 1 teaspoon kosher salt
- 14 oz ground pork
- 1 tablespoon panko breadcrumbs
- 2 medium eggs
- 1/2 teaspoon black pepper
- 1/2 teaspoon grated nutmeg

xxxxxxxxxxxxxxxxxxxxxx

Instructions:

A. Mix flour, milk, yeast, and sugar in a bowl. Knead briefly.
B. Add butter and half the salt. Knead for 10 minutes until smooth.
C. Split dough into 10 balls. Put on a floured sheet, cover with plastic. Let rise for 30 minutes.
D. Mix 1 egg, pork, breadcrumbs, pepper, nutmeg, and remaining salt in another bowl. Divide into 10 parts.
E. Roll each dough ball into an oval, about 1/8 inch thick.
F. Shape pork mix into sausages. Place on dough ovals.
G. Fold the short sides in, then long sides over. Seal seams.
H. Place rolls seam-side down on a lined baking sheet. Cover, let rise for 1 hour.
I. Heat oven to 450°F after 30 minutes.
J. Mix 1 tablespoon of water with the remaining egg. Brush on rolls.
K. Bake for 11-12 minutes until golden. Serve warmly.

Special Notes:

- For extra flavor, try adding a pinch of caraway seeds to the dough.
- To make the rolls even more special, brush them with melted butter right after baking for a glossy finish and richer taste.

21. Dutch Potato Salad

This Dutch potato salad is a hit at picnics. It's a mix of potatoes, peas, and ham with a tangy dressing. The recipe comes from the Netherlands and is similar to Russian Olivier salad. It's easy to make and tastes great cold, perfect for summer meals or potlucks.

Preparation Time: 50 minutes

Serving size: 6 servings

Ingredients:

- 3 cups potatoes, peeled and cut into 1/4" chunks
- 1 tart apple, unpeeled and cubed in 1/4" chunks
- 7 oz ham steak, cut into 1/4" chunks
- 1/2 cup cornichons, cut in 1/4" chunks
- 1 cup green peas
- 1/4 onion, thinly sliced and cut small
- 3 hard-boiled eggs, cut into 1/4" pieces
- 1/2 cup cocktail onions, halved
- 5 tablespoons low-fat mayonnaise
- 1 tablespoon apple cider vinegar
- 1 teaspoon no-salt-added ketchup
- 1/2 teaspoon kosher salt
- 1/4 teaspoon black pepper

xxxxxxxxxxxxxxxxxxxxxxx

Instructions:

A. Cook peas and potatoes in lightly salted boiling water. Once boiling again, turn off heat and let sit for a few minutes to finish cooking.
B. Drain the hot water and add ice-cold water to stop cooking. Drain again and let cool.
C. In a big bowl, mix cooled peas and potatoes with apple, cornichons, ham, cocktail onions, regular onion, and eggs.
D. Make dressing in a small bowl: mix mayonnaise, vinegar, ketchup, salt, and pepper.
E. Pour dressing over the salad and mix well.
F. Put salad on a plate and serve.

Special Notes:

- For extra crunch, add a handful of chopped walnuts or sunflower seeds.
- Try swapping the ham for smoked chicken or turkey for a different flavor twist.

22. Mashed Potato Medley

This Dutch comfort food is a hit in every home. It's a simple mix of potatoes, carrots, and onions that's both filling and tasty. The dish is perfect for cold nights and easy to make. You'll love how the flavors come together in this hearty meal.

Preparation Time: 35 minutes

Serving size: 6 servings

Ingredients:

- 2&1/4 pounds (about 5 cups) potatoes, peeled and chopped
- 1&1/2 pounds (about 4 cups) carrots, peeled and chopped
- 7 large onions, coarsely chopped
- 2 bay leaves
- 1 tablespoon unsalted butter
- 1/4 cup full-fat milk
- 1/4 teaspoon ground nutmeg
- Kosher salt and black pepper to taste

xxxxxxxxxxxxxxxxxxxxxx

Instructions:

A. Peel and chop the potatoes into chunks. Put them in a big pot with water and some salt.
B. Turn on the heat and wait for the water to boil.
C. While waiting, peel and chop the carrots. Add them to the pot with the bay leaves.
D. Peel and chop the onions roughly. Cook them in a pan until they're soft.
E. Add the cooked onions to the pot with potatoes and carrots.
F. When everything is soft, take out the bay leaves.
G. Mash everything together in the pot.
H. Add nutmeg, salt, and pepper. Mix well.
I. Pour in the milk and add the butter. Mash again until it's smooth.
J. It's ready to serve!

Special Notes:

- For a twist, try using sweet potatoes instead of regular ones. It adds a nice sweetness to the dish.
- If you want a smoother texture, use a hand blender instead of mashing by hand. It makes the dish extra creamy.

23. Bacon-Hugged Meat rolls

This Dutch treat is a tasty twist on meatballs. Popular in the Netherlands, these pork rolls snuggle up in bacon blankets. They're easy to make and pack a flavor punch. If you like meaty bites with a crispy outside, you'll love these little guys.

Preparation Time: 20 minutes

Cooking Time: 30 minutes

Serving size: 4 servings

Ingredients:

- 12 slices lean bacon
- 1 cup ground lean pork
- 1 teaspoon kosher salt
- 1/2 teaspoon ground mace
- 1/4 teaspoon black pepper
- 1/4 teaspoon ground nutmeg
- 2 tablespoons dry fine breadcrumbs

xxxxxxxxxxxxxxxxxxxxxx

Instructions:

A. Heat your oven to 350°F.
B. In a bowl, mix the ground pork, salt, breadcrumbs, mace, pepper, and nutmeg.
C. Shape the mix into 4 long rolls, like mini logs.
D. Wrap each roll with 3 bacon slices. Tuck the ends under.
E. Stick a toothpick at each end to hold the bacon in place.
F. Put the rolls on a baking sheet.
G. Bake for 30 minutes until the bacon is crispy.
H. Take out the toothpicks before you serve.

Special Notes:

- For extra juicy rolls, soak the breadcrumbs in a splash of milk before mixing them in.
- Try brushing the bacon with maple syrup before baking for a sweet and salty kick. It'll make the outside extra crispy and give a nice glaze.

24. Mustard Magic Soup

This Dutch soup is a crowd-pleaser. It's creamy, tangy, and full of flavor. The mix of mustards gives it a kick, while the bacon adds a smoky touch. It's perfect for cold days or when you want something different. You'll love how easy it is to make and how good it tastes.

Preparation Time: 35 minutes

Serving size: 4 servings

Ingredients:

- 4 oz slab bacon, cut into matchsticks
- 4&1/4 cups chicken stock
- 1 medium shallot, finely chopped
- 3&1/2 tablespoons unsalted butter
- 1 tablespoon grainy mustard
- 1 tablespoon smooth mustard
- 1/2 cup all-purpose flour, sifted
- 1/2 teaspoon mustard seeds
- 1/2 cup heavy cream
- Kosher salt and ground pepper to taste
- Chopped chives for garnish

xxxxxxxxxxxxxxxxxxxxxx

Instructions:

A. Cook the bacon in a pan over medium heat until crispy. Set aside on paper towels.
B. In a pot, cook the shallot in butter until soft.
C. Stir in mustard seeds and both types of mustard.
D. Add flour and mix well. Slowly pour in the chicken stock, stirring to make a smooth sauce. Cook for 1-2 minutes.
E. Pour in the cream. Add salt and pepper to your liking.
F. Serve the soup in bowls. Top with chives and crispy bacon.

Special Notes:

- For extra depth, try roasting the mustard seeds before adding them to the soup. It brings out a nuttier flavor.
- If you like it spicier, add a dash of hot sauce or a pinch of cayenne pepper to the soup. It'll give your taste buds a surprise kick!

25. Cheesy Puff Pockets

These tasty treats were born in Dutch snack bars during the 1960s. They're quick, easy, and super popular in the Netherlands. Crispy on the outside, gooey on the inside - perfect for cheese lovers! You'll get hooked on these little golden squares filled with melty Gouda goodness.

Preparation Time: 20 minutes

Serving size: 5 servings

Ingredients:

- 5 sheets puff pastry (9" x 14" each)
- 10 slices Gouda cheese
- 2 large eggs
- 2 cups breadcrumbs
- Water as needed
- Sunflower oil for frying

xxxxxxxxxxxxxxxxxxxxx

Instructions:

A. Heat sunflower oil to 350°F in a deep fryer or heavy pot.
B. Cut puff pastry sheets in half. Trim Gouda slices to fit on half of each pastry rectangle, leaving about 1/4-inch space around the edges.
C. Stack 2-3 cheese slices on each pastry half.
D. Dab water on pastry edges. Top with remaining pastry rectangles and press edges to seal.
E. Set up two shallow dishes: one with beaten eggs, one with breadcrumbs.
F. Dip each pastry pocket in egg, then coat with breadcrumbs.
G. Fry in batches until golden brown on both sides, flipping once.
H. Drain on paper towels and serve hot.

Special Notes:

- For extra crunch, mix some crushed potato chips into the breadcrumbs.
- Try adding a thin slice of ham or a sprinkle of dried herbs between the cheese layers for a flavor twist.

Enjoy Delicious Dutch Desserts

xxxxxxxxxxxxxxxxxxxxx

26. Dutch Spice Cookies

These cookies are a Christmas hit in the Netherlands. They're also loved in Belgium and parts of Germany. The mix of spices makes them taste great. You'll enjoy the crisp texture and warm flavors. They're perfect with a cup of tea or coffee.

Preparation Time: 2 hours

Serving size: 3 dozen

Ingredients:

- 1&3/4 cups all-purpose flour
- 2 teaspoons ground cinnamon
- 1/2 teaspoon baking soda
- 1/2 teaspoon kosher salt
- 1/2 teaspoon ground nutmeg
- 1/2 teaspoon ground cloves
- 1/4 teaspoon ground ginger
- 1/4 teaspoon ground pepper
- 1/2 cup brown sugar
- 6 tablespoons unsalted butter, softened
- 1/4 cup whole milk

xxxxxxxxxxxxxxxxxxxxxx

Instructions:

A. Beat the butter in a big bowl until it's soft.
B. Mix in brown sugar. Beat for 1-2 minutes until smooth.
C. In another bowl, mix flour, salt, spices, and baking soda.
D. Add this dry mix to the butter mix. Stir well.
E. Pour in the milk. Mix until you get wet crumbs. Use your hands to make a soft dough.
F. Wrap the dough and chill it for 30 minutes to 1 hour.
G. Heat the oven to 350°F.
H. Roll out the chilled dough to 1/4 - 1/3 inch thick. Cut cookies with a 2 1/2 inch cutter.
I. Put cookies on a baking sheet.
J. Bake for 11-12 minutes until the edges start to brown. While the first batch bakes, reshape and cut the leftover dough.
K. Let cookies cool on the sheet for a minute, then move to a wire rack.
L. Repeat until all dough is used. Enjoy your cookies!

Special Notes:

- Try adding a pinch of cardamom to the spice mix for an extra layer of flavor.
- For a fun twist, press a whole almond into the center of each cookie before baking. This adds crunch and makes them look like traditional Dutch "speculaas" cookies.

27. Dutch Doughnuts

These Dutch doughnuts, called Oliebollen, are a hit in the Netherlands. They're round, crispy on the outside, and soft inside. People love them for their sweet taste and sugar coating. You'll find them at fairs and during New Year's. They're easy to make and fun to eat!

Preparation Time: 2 hours (including rising time)

Serving size: 48-60 doughnuts

Ingredients:

- 2 cups lukewarm milk, plus extra if needed
- 1 (0.25 oz) package active dry yeast
- 3 tablespoons granulated sugar
- 4 cups all-purpose flour
- 1 pinch kosher salt
- 1 large egg
- 2 quarts vegetable oil, for frying
- Powdered sugar, for dusting

xxxxxxxxxxxxxxxxxxxxxxx

Instructions:

A. Mix milk, sugar, and yeast in a small bowl. Let it sit for 8-10 minutes.
B. In a big bowl, sift flour and salt. Make a hole in the middle.
C. Crack the egg into the hole. Pour in the yeast mix.
D. Beat with a mixer. Add more milk if needed. Cover the bowl.
E. Let the batter rise in a warm spot for 1-2 hours.
F. Heat oil to 350°F in a deep pan.
G. Use two wet spoons to drop small balls of batter into the hot oil.
H. Fry each batch for about 6 minutes. Flip halfway through.
I. Put fried doughnuts on paper towels to drain.
J. Dust with powdered sugar and serve warm.

Special Notes:

- For extra flavor, add a teaspoon of vanilla extract or some lemon zest to the batter.
- Try mixing in some raisins or chopped apples for a fruity twist. Just fold them in gently before frying.

28. Brandied Apricots

This old French treat is a hit at parties. People love these sweet, boozy apricots. They're easy to make and taste great. You just need dried apricots, sugar, and brandy. They're perfect with ice cream or on their own. Once you try them, you'll want to make them again and again.

Preparation Time: 30 minutes (plus 24 hours soaking time)

Serving size: 15 servings

Ingredients:

- 4 cups dried apricots
- 1 2/3 cups water
- 1 cup granulated sugar
- 1 lemon, zested
- 1 cup fruit brandy

xxxxxxxxxxxxxxxxxxxxx

Instructions:

A. Wash the dried apricots.
B. Put apricots in a big pot. Add water and sugar.
C. Let them soak for a day.
D. After soaking, add lemon zest to the pot.
E. Boil the mix. Take out the apricots and put them in jars.
F. Cook the leftover liquid until it gets thick.
G. Take the pot off the heat. Let it cool a bit.
H. Pour in the brandy. Take out the lemon zest.
I. Pour the syrup over the apricots in jars. Shake them a little.
J. Close the jars tight. Keep them in a dark, cool place for 6 weeks before eating or giving as gifts.

Special Notes:

- For a twist, try using different types of brandy like apple or pear. It'll give a unique flavor to your apricots.
- If you like it spicy, add a cinnamon stick or a few cloves to the syrup while it's cooking. Just remember to remove them before jarring.

29. Classic Dutch Almond Crisps

These thin, crunchy cookies are a Dutch favorite. Made with almonds and cinnamon, they're named after Belgian lace for their delicate look. They're easy to make and perfect with coffee or tea. You'll love how they melt in your mouth!

Preparation Time: 40 minutes + 2 hours resting time

Serving size: 48 cookies

Ingredients:

- 10 cups all-purpose flour
- 7 cups chopped almonds
- 3&1/4 cups (26 oz) unsalted butter
- 6 cups granulated sugar
- 4&1/2 tablespoons ground cinnamon
- 5 teaspoons kosher salt
- 2 cups water

xxxxxxxxxxxxxxxxxxxxxx

Instructions:

A. Melt the butter in a large pot.
B. Add water, salt, sugar, and cinnamon to the melted butter. Mix well.
C. Stir in the flour until combined.
D. Gently fold in the chopped almonds.
E. Let the dough sit for 2 hours.
F. Heat your oven to 350°F.
G. Drop small spoonfuls of dough onto lined baking sheets.
H. Cover with plastic wrap and press each cookie flat.
I. Take off the wrap and bake for 6-8 minutes.
J. Let cookies cool on a wire rack before serving.

Special Notes:

- For extra crunch, try toasting the almonds before adding them to the dough.
- Dip half of each cooled cookie in melted dark chocolate for a fancy twist on this classic treat.

30. Dutch Almond Butter Cake

This yummy cake comes from the Netherlands. It's a hit there and people love it. The cake is soft and moist with a nice almond taste. It's easy to make and great for sharing with friends or family. You'll want to have more than one slice!

Preparation Time: 15 minutes

Cooking Time: 30 minutes

Serving Size: 16 servings

Ingredients:

- 2&1/2 cups all-purpose flour
- 2 teaspoons baking powder
- 1 tablespoon pure almond extract
- 1 cup (8 oz) unsalted butter, softened
- 1&1/2 cups white sugar
- 2 medium eggs, beaten

xxxxxxxxxxxxxxxxxxxxx

Instructions:

A. Turn on your oven to 350°F (175°C). Grease two 8-inch round pans.
B. In a big bowl, mix the soft butter and sugar.
C. Use a hand mixer until it's light and fluffy.
D. Add the beaten eggs to the bowl. Mix well.
E. Pour in the almond extract. Stir it in.
F. In another bowl, mix the flour and baking powder.
G. Add the flour mix to the butter mix. Stir with a spoon until you get a thick dough.
H. Split the dough between the two pans. Press it down evenly.
I. Bake for about 30 minutes. The tops should look golden brown.
J. Take the cakes out and let them cool a bit. Then slice and enjoy!

Special Notes:

- Try adding a pinch of salt to the dough. It might sound weird, but it can make the almond flavor pop even more!
- If you want to make it extra special, sprinkle some sliced almonds on top before baking. They'll get nice and toasty in the oven.

Conclusion

Now that you've explored these Dutch recipes, you're ready to bring the flavors of the Netherlands into your own kitchen. Dutch cuisine offers a wonderful mix of comfort foods and unique tastes that are sure to please your family and friends.

Remember, Dutch cooking is all about simplicity and hearty flavors. You can easily add these dishes to your regular meal rotation. Try starting your day with a Dutch-style breakfast like Apple Bacon Pancakes or Gingerbread Waffles. On colder days, warm up with a comforting Dutch stew or soup.

Don't forget to experiment with Dutch seafood dishes. The recipes for herring and mussels will introduce you to new and delicious ways of preparing fish.

Potatoes and pasta play a big role in Dutch cooking, and you'll find they bring a special comfort to many dishes. And of course, save room for dessert! Treats like Windmill Cookies and Brandied Apricots are perfect for ending a meal or sharing with guests.

As you cook your way through these recipes, you'll discover the joy of Dutch home cooking. Each dish tells a story of Dutch culture and tradition. Whether you're making a quick weeknight dinner or preparing a feast for friends, these recipes will help you create memorable meals.

So, grab your apron and start cooking! Share these tasty Dutch dishes with your loved ones and spread the love for Dutch cuisine. Happy cooking!

Dear Reader,

I want to express my sincere gratitude for downloading and dedicating your time to reading my book. It means the world to me that you chose to invest your valuable time in exploring the content I have shared. I truly hope that you found the information beneficial and that you had an enjoyable reading experience.

As an author, my primary goal is to impart my knowledge and insights to others. I recognize that there is an overwhelming number of e-books available, and I am deeply honored that you decided to give mine a chance. Your decision to read my work reflects your commitment to personal growth and learning, and I am thrilled to have played a role in your journey.

If you could spare a moment to provide an honest review or feedback about my book, I would be incredibly grateful. Your opinions and suggestions are invaluable to my development as a writer. They help me understand what resonates with readers and inspire me to create even more valuable content in the future. Who knows, your feedback might even spark the idea for my next book!

Once again, thank you for your support and dedication. It means more to me than words can express.

Martha Stanford

Printed in Great Britain
by Amazon